Design and Make

Greetings Cards

Jan and Ted Arundell

J M Dent & Sons Ltd London

The authors would like to thank all
those who have helped to make this
publication possible, in particular
Brian Yale, of Group One Four, T. A.
Shenstone, Tony Greaves-Lord, Ron
Welsh and M. Myers & Son Ltd.

Annie Whitaker's skill and patience
in sorting out and typing the
manuscript are very much appreciated.

First published 1975

Made in Great Britain
for J. M. DENT & SONS LTD
Aldine House · Albemarle Street · London

Filmset by BAS Printers Limited, Wallop,
Hampshire

ISBN 0 460 04122 3

Contents

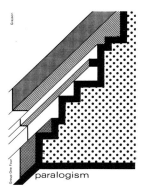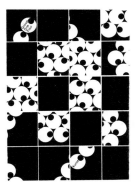

1a–d

paralogism

false in point or form; contrary to logical rules.

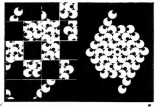

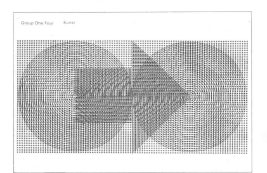

1f

paralogism

false in point or form; contrary to logical rules.

1e

1g

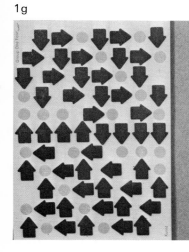

1h

Introduction

When we consider our highly commercialized Christmas, with all the extra personnel employed by the Post Office to deliver the millions of cards sent annually, it is difficult to believe that the custom of sending Christmas cards originated only just over 100 years ago. Valentines have been sent for centuries, but not quite as we know them. Originally they were beautifully written letters, verses or decorated lover's knots or even gifts, and they were a serious declaration of the sender's feelings.

The idea of the Valentine appealed to the sentimental Victorians and rapidly increased in popularity. Home made and commercially made cards were similar, often being a collage of all kinds of laces, ribbons, silk flowers etc. The more exotic ones were composed of many layers and had padded centres on which the message was inscribed. The card was often so thick and elaborate that a special box contained it. Trick cards were a speciality of the period, with little doors, windows and other moving parts (some quite complicated, mechanically) which, when opened or moved, were found to conceal little drawings or sentiments.

The invention of the Christmas card increased the scope for sending sentimental messages. A card of this nature was appropriate to send to all one's friends and relatives. The early Christmas cards were identical to the Valentine with the addition of 'A Merry Christmas' or similar message. It took some little time for the separate styles to evolve.

With the advent of colour printing a flood of little coloured scraps appeared which could be cut up and used for decorating all manner of objects, including greetings cards. There were pictures of flowers, animals, people and little decorated sentiments, and they proved to be a great novelty until well into the twentieth century. The Americans bought large quantities especially for making cards.

From the beginning there was a wide range of materials available, and designing and making one's own cards was a popular craft. The Victorians had to manage with flour paste instead of our fabulous range of adhesives, but this did not stop them from making large quantities of elaborate cards.

The fashion of card sending has grown in popularity and today we have cards for all manner of occasions (see p. 62), and at every stage in the history of the card there have been people who were prepared to take the trouble to design and make their own. As various techniques have come into fashion, they have been adapted to this purpose. Pin prick decoration on paper was popular during the last century and was often used to decorate cards. Water-colour work was much used at the beginning of this century and now we encourage the development of a wealth of techniques, most of which are suitable for making cards.

It is often argued that the sending of greetings cards is a waste of time and money, especially in the great quantities that are purchased today. Nevertheless their popularity grows and we continue to seek new reasons for sending cards. Some may be a little fatuous, but we are always delighted to know that someone has remembered us.

As it is so easy to wander down the road to the local shop and choose one's card from the wide selection available, one wonders — why bother to make them?

There are several reasons why. How many times do we look at a family's Christmas display and see several cards from different people, all identical except for the signature. The specially designed card is never like any other and it indicates, through its individuality and the time and care taken over its preparation, that the maker/sender is very sincere in his good wishes. What is more, he has the satisfaction of making something that is peculiarly his — no small consideration in an age of mass production.

The nature of present day occupations leaves many of us with the need of creative outlets. We have shorter working weeks and more spare time. With so much leisure we feel the need to develop skills that are quite different from those we use at work. Hence the increase in popularity of crafts and do-it-yourself skills, all of which enable people to make things they need and satisfy their innate creative urge. The making of greetings cards falls into this category, offering a great deal of pleasure and satisfaction to individuals who work on their own and to families who like to work as a group.

Another incentive is the price. The better designed greetings card has become so expensive that it is well worth the trouble to make one's own. Dozens of cards can be made for a fraction of the price of a few bought ones.

This book is intended as a guide to students, teachers, parents, youth leaders and individuals who wish to know how to start to make cards and how to develop any skills they may already have.

American terms are given in square brackets where they differ from the British.

2 Victorian Valentine card reproduced by
permission of T. A. Shenstone. It was sent
by his grandfather to his grandmother.

Basic Equipment

a *Scissors.* One really sharp pair is essential. Poor, blunt-edged scissors without sharp points are soul destroying to use if a neat, crisp result is required. So don't try to manage if you haven't got a good pair. Invest in one. It's money well spent. You won't need a large pair — an overall length of 130 mm [5–6 ins] will be big enough.

b *A metal ruler and a rigid-backed razor blade or handyman's knife.* These will be needed to cut your cards into the neat, crisp shape that gives them their really professional look. Always cut on top of an old piece of cardboard, wood or thick newspaper to protect the table. Metal rules must be kept clean or they may mark the paper.

c *A metal or plastic set square* for making sure that all the corners of a rectangular card are 90°.

d *A drawing pen,* which need only be one of the old fashioned wooden handles fitted with a cheap, straight writing nib to give excellent results. Some fountain pens are very nice for drawing and if you are feeling affluent, one of the expensive draughtsman's pens with a circular nib such as the Rotring [Rapidograph] or Pelican pen is really worth having.

e *Other items* which you may need from time to time include a pair of compasses, needles of various sizes, brushes and felt-tipped pens.

Materials

a *Stiff paper or thin cardboard* from which to make the greetings card itself. Do not try to economize here, for this could mean that you may never achieve a professional finish.

b *Adhesive.* Most work with greetings cards is of a fairly detailed nature, so adhesive that is packed in a tube with a fine nozzle will help you to make a neat job. P.V.A. adhesives like Marvin [Elmer's glue] or a rapid drying adhesive like Bostik No. 1 [Sobo] are recommended as they dry to a clear film which does not show too badly should it appear on the face of the work. Both these adhesives will fix all the items mentioned in this book. Cheaper office pastes and wallpaper pastes are useful, but only for fixing paper to paper. Rubber-based adhesives like Copydex [Best-test] are excellent where fabrics are used. Platignum produce a pen-like tool filled with adhesive. It is called a 'spot stick' [the American equivalent is a glue pen made by Pastemaker] and is unbeatable for applying small spots of adhesive exactly where they are required. Always read the instructions supplied with the

adhesive and use only as recommended.

All other materials are subject to personal preference, therefore are not itemized, but a list of suppliers at the end of the book is given to help you with some of your purchases.

Making the Card Structure

There are three methods of constructing a card.

Either The structure is made first and the design/picture is made directly onto it, *or* the picture is made and a suitable card structure is made afterwards to support it, *or* a combination of the two, where the design and the card are inseparable, as on page 50.

Whichever way you choose to work, sooner or later you will need to know how to cut and fold paper/cardboard so that you can obtain professional results. No matter how good your pictorial ideas, they will never look convincing unless your cards are crisp, clean and neat.

Greetings cards should be made from paper which will not bend under its own weight, so that the cards will stand freely on their own or propped against a wall.

Making a perfect fold in a piece of paper/cardboard

Stiff paper/cardboard
Ruler (preferably metal)
Pencil
Sharp knife
Cutting pad

Using a ruler as a guide, draw a faint pencil line on the paper/cardboard where you wish the fold to occur i.e. on the outside of the fold to be. Hold the ruler in place along the pencil line and, using it as a guide, cut with a knife *half way through* the paper/cardboard where the pencil line is marked. This is called 'scoring'.

The paper/cardboard will now bend easily and cleanly along this line, away from the cut. To make the fold very sharp, run the back of the finger nail, or a piece of plastic, along it. Practise making folds like this. In order to make the paper/cardboard fold the reverse way, score the other side of the paper. By alternating sides, you can make a zig-zag greetings card.

Trimming the edges of a rectangular card

Folded greetings card
Ruler (metal)
Pencil
Knife
Set Square

Having chosen the size of paper/ cardboard and folded it, make sure that the top and particularly the bottom edges of the greetings card are at right angles (90°) to the fold, otherwise the card will not stand upright. Put the folded card flat on an old table or board and place the set square as in diagram (4a), making sure the left-hand edge of the square lines up exactly with the left-hand edge of the card. Mark lightly line A–B and then repeat process as in diagram (4b). Then cut away surplus at A–B and C–D using metal ruler and knife and making a very clean cut through both layers. Now the third side B–D can be marked and cut as in the diagram, provided that the set square is lined up neatly with A–B or C–D before marking and cutting.

Mounting a picture on a card

Test the picture in various positions on the card and decide on the most satisfactory position in which to fix it. Apply adhesive to the back of the picture – just four very tiny spots, one in each corner – then press firmly into position on the card. A large picture may need a little more adhesive, maybe one or two spots along each side. Never spread adhesive over the whole of the back of the picture as this will upset the tension between the two sheets and the result will be lumpy and messy looking. There is no way to remedy this once it has occurred.

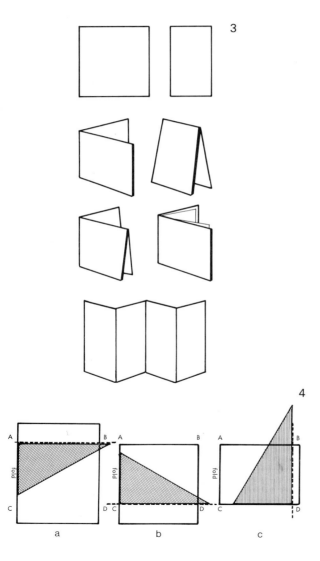

3

4

a   b   c

Paper Collage

The shapes used in the first set of cards (figs. 6–8) were cut from a paper printed with a small triangular pattern, which was used as a guide to cut a number of heart shapes of varying sizes. With a little juggling and a tiny suggestion of drawing, it was possible to come up with a Valentine card, a Christmas card and a little boy's Birthday card. A little more effort and we could no doubt have a floral Mother's Day card and possibly a few Easter chickens.

The designs for cards (figs. 9–12) are more closely related to the original pattern of the paper which was, rather surprisingly, of a very symmetrical and geometric nature. By cutting out odd bits of the pattern and re-assembling them in rather unexpected ways, it was possible to arrive at a collection of designs with an Art Deco flavour which would be suitable for any cheerful greeting, invitation or 'thank you' message.

The third collection (figs. 13–15) shows three interpretations of the inexhaustible Christmas tree theme. Two of the designs are basically a triangle and the third a parallelogram. Could further tree designs be made from other geometric shapes?

Wrapping paper

Pieces of wrapping paper
Scissors
Adhesive
Stiff mounting paper

optional:
Pen and ink

Writing in 1960, Vance Packard bewailed the amount of rubbish thrown away by the average American family. Christmas is one of our most wasteful periods. Every year we destroy quantities of boxes, envelopes, ribbons, fancy string, cartons and expensive coloured wrapping paper, much of which could be re-used to great advantage.

On the following three pages you will see examples of cards (figs. 6–12) made from three different designs of wrapping paper. The most useful papers to collect are a) plain coloured, b) textured and c) paper with simple geometric patterns.

5

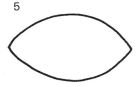 

6

7

8

12

9–12

13, 14

15

14

Old magazines

Old magazines
Scissors
Adhesive
Mounting card or stiff paper

This set of cards is made from pieces of coloured paper cut from magazine illustrations. Today's magazines tempt us with a wealth of colour printing which, when cut up, gives us not only good colour, but an endless variety of rich texture, the like of which would be difficult to obtain from any other source — certainly not from specially purchased coloured paper.

On close inspection it will be found that the shapes from which the pictures are built are very simple, and of limited variety on each card. The rich effect is obtained by contrasting different tones and textures. The cards illustrated depict wintry scenes suitable for Christmas, but this technique can be used for making all kinds of pictures.

16–18

Sequin Collage

19, 20

A collection of sequins
Adhesive (Platignum Spot Stick)
[Pastemaker glue pen]
Mounting card

optional:
Paint brush
Spring washers (fig. 19)
Stick-on letter labels (fig. 20).

The range of sequins, ribbons, buttons, tapes, threads, beads etc., found in the haberdashery [notions] department of a large store will make possible an endless permutation of designs.

Sequins, the main element in these two cards, are obtainable in all colours and many shapes. As they are light and electrostatic, a small, dampened paint brush, or a sharpened wax crayon, is useful for picking them up individually. Do not use a cellulose adhesive for holding them in place, as it will contaminate the metal finish. The Spot Stick is suitable for fine work and causes no damage to the sequins or to similarly finished metallic papers.

The message was made up of stick-on labels (obtainable from any good stationery shop).

When you have learned how to handle these materials you will be able to make your own range of designs from similar items.

Wallpaper Collage

Scraps of flocked [textured]
wallpaper
Sequins
Scissors
Adhesive
Mounting card

Wallpaper scraps are easily obtained.
Wallpaper is manufactured in such a
wide variety of designs, colours and
finishes that it offers endless
opportunity for original work.

Figs. 21–23 were designed in a
similar manner to those on p. 13,
with the addition of a few sequins
to add crispness to the shapes.

21–3

Wallpaper Collage

Wallpaper
Metallic wrapping paper
Sequins
Adhesive
Various mounting cards

Careful study of scraps of wallpaper will reveal a wealth of simple shapes which can be cut out and re-assembled on plain or metallic paper to make all kinds of cards. The Christening card (fig. 27), was made from two kinds of stripe, a circular motif and some star-shaped flowers, all cut from two Sanderson wall-papers. The shapes were mounted on two colours of pink card and a few pearl sequins were added as a finishing touch.

Figs. 28–30 are formal, religious designs made from a combination of metallic papers, flocked [textured] wallpapers and sequins arranged in such a way that the results simulate the richness of altar cloths. The centre of fig. 29 is composed of two spring washers superimposed to look like a mounted jewel.

These examples give just a hint of the infinite variety of cards that can be made with this material.

24—6

27

28

29, 30

21

Seed Collage

Explore the jars in the kitchen and see if their contents would be suitable for making a mosaic-like pattern. Dried peas and beans are useful and nowadays there is a good range of pasta. You can dry your own melon seeds by leaving them on a sunny window ledge and turning them each day.

Arranging the design is simple if you tip your collection of items onto a piece of graph paper and push them around with the end of a small paint brush or knitting needle rather than with your fingers. When the design is satisfactory, it is glued into place and mounted on the card as you wish. The small glue pen is recommended for this fine work.

Split peas
Lentils
Whole peppers
Spaghetti rings
Adhesive (Platignum Spot Stick)
[Pastemaker glue pen]
Mounting card

With a little practice you may be able to design without the aid of the graph paper as used in figs. 31–33.

31–3

34

Melon seeds
Cocktail sticks
Pen and ink
Adhesive (Platignum Spot Stick)
[Pastemaker glue pen]
Mounting card

Cards 34–37 are made by the same technique, but with the addition of a little pen and ink drawing. Further variation can be obtained by colouring melon seeds with ink or textile dyes.

35–7

38

39–41

Stickers

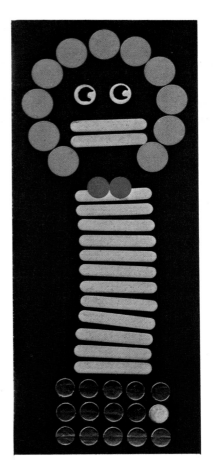

Self adhesive stickers
Coloured paper

optional:
Instant dry lettering for Mother's Day
card (see p. 59)
Pen and ink

This is a medium which even a small
child can manipulate and with it
obtain results which are clean and
professional. Good stationery shops
stock both paper and vinyl sticker
labels in a very wide selection of
shapes and colours. When peeled
off their protective backing film, they
will stick to most surfaces including
paper. The designs illustrated give
only the merest hint of the potential
of this medium.

42

43

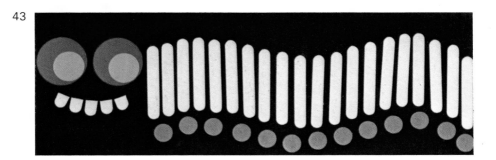

Instant Dry Colour

is quite expensive but it gives superb flat areas of brilliant colour of a quality very difficult to obtain by any other means.

Dry colour film
Dry colour stylus or very sharp knife (preferably a scalpel) for cutting colour
Pair of compasses and/or ruler
Thick cardboard or paper for protecting table
Shiny card for mounting

optional:
Sequins and washers

Dry colour is obtainable from art suppliers. (In the USA dry colour is available under the brand names Bourges and Letraset 'Letra film', 'Letratone' and 'Letracolor'). It is a very thin sheet of semi-transparent colour which is so frail that it is mounted on a backing sheet of plastic for support. The unsupported side is sticky and is protected by waxy paper which must be kept next to the colour at all times prior to fixing the colour film in its final position, otherwise the colour will pick up dust and lose its adhesive powers. Compared with other methods of colouring, dry colour

Once you have decided on the shapes you wish to cut from the sheet of dry colour, you will find that a patient, clean, workman-like approach is all that is required to obtain first class results. Place the dry colour, sticky side down, protective sheet underneath, on a thick piece of cardboard, and with the stylus (or sharp knife) make a clean cut through the colour and its supporting sheet. Cuts can be made free-hand, against a ruler or other guide, or the stylus may be held in a pair of school-type compasses and circles cut out as in fig. 47. The cut pieces are lifted from the protective film and placed in position on the shiny mounting card from which your card is to be made. Juggle them around until you are satisfied with the arrangement, then, with a blunt instrument (back of finger nail or end of rounded paintbrush handle), rub the surface of the dry colour gently, until it changes colour slightly. Now it will be possible to put the blade of a sharp knife between the colour and its supporting film and carefully lever away the latter. When all the supporting film has been removed, place a sheet of the protective paper over the design and burnish the whole thing gently with a blunt instrument. This will make the pieces stick firmly in place, resulting in a design built up from impeccable layers of colour.

44

45, 46

47

It is advisable to use this material as economically as possible and inspection of the cards illustrated will show how all the shapes cut from one piece of colour can be utilized, each design being made up from a small area of material.

The shape used to create fig. 44 was an oblong cut up freely into a number of triangles. A circle was drawn on the card to guide the laying out of the colour. The design was finished with a centre of metallic paper. Fig. 45 was made from a number of concentric circles and some of the supporting film. Fig. 47 was cut from a piece shaped like a segment of a circle.

By overlapping the colour film a variety of tonal and chromatic variations can be achieved.

48, 49

Dry colour and wallpaper
These designs utilize the techniques
described in detail on pp. 17, 18 and 26.

Drawing

Pen and ink

Pair of compasses fitted with pencil
Drawing ink and pen
Rubber [Eraser]
Scissors
Smooth white paper (good quality
writing paper will do)
Coloured mounting paper
Adhesive

The circular 'flowers' which are the
basis of all the designs shown here,
are very simple to make. Anyone
who has the doodling tendency, and
cannot resist decorating covers of
exercise books and telephone
directories, will soon learn how to
create these in an endless array of
patterns.

Using the compasses, draw a number
of unequally spaced concentric
circles on smooth white paper. The
outer circle will determine the size of
the 'flower head'. With pen and
drawing ink, start a doodle pattern
at the centre of the circles, always
using a long, continuous line, never
a sketchy, broken one, and wherever
the shapes are intended to join up,
make sure that they do so neatly. Do

not try to rush the work. When the
design is complete and the ink dry,
carefully cut out the shape on the
outside of the outer line. (You will
soon learn that certain shapes are
easier to cut out than others, and
you will design accordingly.) Using
a soft rubber, clean off the pencil
guide lines.

There are endless ways in which
these designs can be mounted, either
using them singly or in groups.
Figs. 51—54 show four quite
different ideas to start you off, all
mounted on two tones of stiff paper
except for the square 'garden'. These
are all very feminine cards suitable
for Mother's Day, Easter Day or a
christening.

51–3

54

31

55

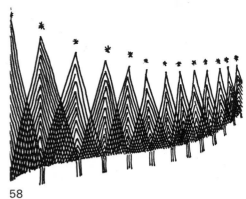

58

56

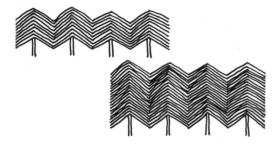

57

Parallel lines

Drawing ink and pen or felt-tipped pen
Smooth paper

Now that you have practised doodling, you will find that parallel line drawings follow without too much difficulty. This technique is a useful way of achieving the effect of movement or depth in a drawing. Do not attempt to represent items in a naturalistic way, but draw a simplified, stylized shape and follow it repeatedly with line after line, until a rhythmic, almost geometric pattern is built up.

The two Christmas tree designs are constructed from an upturned 'v', and give an indication of the amount of variation that can be achieved by very simple means. Subjects that lend themselves to this kind of treatment are grasses in the wind, trees, skies, water and smoke. Look at Van Gogh's paintings of fields of corn.

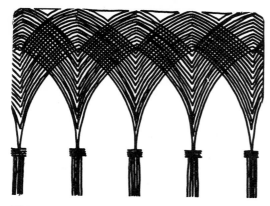

59

Geometrical

A pair of compasses fitted with a
pencil
Ruler
Drawing ink and pen or felt-tipped
pen
Rubber [Eraser]

The designs on these cards were first
constructed with compasses and ruler
and the detailing was a free-hand
line. Try out some of your own ideas.

60

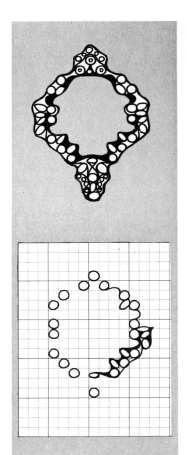

Graph paper

Graph paper, printed on one side only
Pen and ink
Coloured and/or metallic mounting
card
Adhesive

optional:
Instant dry lettering

On p. 30 a circular grid was used as
a drawing guide. The border patterns
are constructed in a similar manner,
but on the back of a piece of graph
paper. The square grid can usually
be seen through the paper sufficiently
to give a guide, and when the
drawing is complete and cut out, the
pen lines camouflage the grid. The
result is a drawing that looks far
more intricate and complicated than
it actually is. After cutting out and
mounting on coloured card, lettering
may be added as described on
pp. 54–9. All kinds of paper are
useful as a starter for this kind of
design, even ordinary lined exercise
paper is useful.

61

62

63, 64

Mechanical

Drawing instruments e.g. ruler, pair of compasses, set square, protractor
Drawing toys e.g. Spirograph, Spirotot etc.
Drawing pens, pencils etc.
Smooth surfaced card

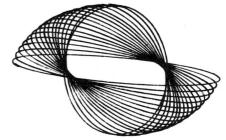

65

Children are fond of drawing with rulers and compasses and sometimes come up with unusual and attractive designs as well as the six-petalled daisy patterns which are the pride and joy of every beginner.

With practice, this activity can be developed into a creative pastime. The work is satisfying and the results can be most elegant and very suitable for all manner of greetings cards. The drawing media can include

66

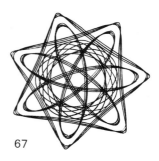

67

pencils, crayons, ball point pens and
ink, the latter preferably in a
draughtsman's compass for circles
(see fig. 65).

Spirograph is a versatile drawing toy
that can be used by people of any
age. It is sold complete with ball
point pens and paper and detailed
instructions for use. There is a
simpler version called Spirotot for
the small child. Both may be used by
a number of people at the same time.

Cards 70 and 71 were produced, to
his own designs, with a creative toy
devised by Tony Greaves-Lord.

68, 69 *Spirograph cards designed and made by Chris, aged seventeen.*

70, 71

Printmaking

One of the advantages of print-making is that effective results can be achieved quickly. To practise, mix some thick colour on a palette or plate, dip one finger into the colour and then print the finger on the paper. Try making a row of prints, then various patterns, dipping the finger in the colour between each print to ensure an even quality of colour all the time. If the print is blotchy and messy, it is because the paint is not thick enough; it should have the consistency of really thick cream.

What can be made with this print? Can you build a flower, stone wall, a set of Christmas tree decorations, a clown's face or a tree top like the one on the right in fig. 72?

Now try printing with the edge of a piece of card. You will find that you can make many textured surfaces.

Scraps

Bits of scrap cardboard, wood, cork, bottle tops, polystyrene [Styrofoam] and anything else to hand.
Thickly mixed paint — powder/ acrylic/poster etc.
Paper with an absorbent rather than shiny surface
Scissors
Adhesive
Mounting card

73

74

Next, roll up a piece of card so that the ends are circular, or if the card is a bit stiff and the shape small, the card may crack, giving you a more angular shape. Cut the end of the shape flat and, using it like a rubber stamp, see how many shapes and images you can print with it.

The row of trees was made from a combination of card and finger prints. Could you make a row of houses using the same technique?

Then try printing with any scrap bits and pieces you can find and soon you will have lots of ideas for cards for any season.

Both these cards were made as described on the previous page with the addition of a little pen and ink drawing.

The outside of the sun was printed from a piece of wood, using two slightly varying colours, and the centre was printed or stippled with an almost dry brush.

The pattern on the second card was started by printing an absolutely regular grid of circles with a cork, to give the bodies of the chicks. The heads are a series of finger prints placed irregularly on the side of the cork shapes and the tiny bit of drawing was added when the printing was dry.

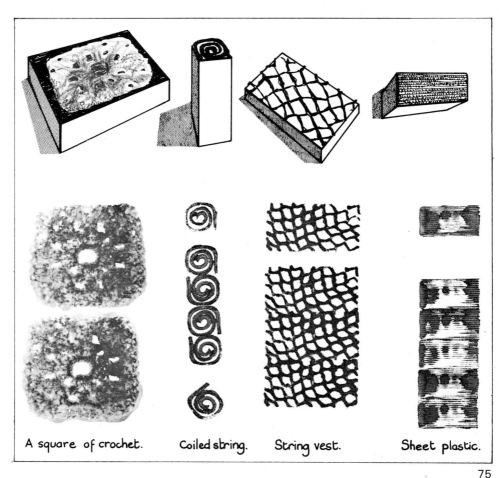

A square of crochet.   Coiled string.   String vest.   Sheet plastic.

Blockmaking

Scraps of string, textiles and sheet plastic etc.
Small pieces of wood, hardboard etc.
Waterproof adhesive (Bostik No. 1) [Sobo]

There are lots of materials such as coils of string, sheet plastic and various textiled textiles e.g. lace, which make delightful prints, but are difficult to manage because of their floppy nature.

To overcome this difficulty, stick the material securely onto a scrap of wood or hardboard, thus forming a printing block. Try to avoid the production of a repetitive pattern. By freely manipulating the block it is possible to produce unexpected and interesting results.

Printmaking

This card was designed and made by
Ray Southwell. The bodies of the
figures were printed partly by the
off-set roller method described in
Design and Make Prints by Jan
Arundell and Ray Southwell, and
partly from blocks like those illustrated on the previous page. The
design was completed with a little
pen and ink drawing.

Rubbings

Wax Crayons or
Heel ball (obtainable in brown and
black and sometimes silver and gold,
from cobblers)
Thin paper (white or coloured)
Textured surfaces
Mounting card
Knife
Ruler

Go for a walk, taking with you some
dark coloured wax crayons (or heel
ball) and some thin paper. You will
see many different textured surfaces —
stones, bricks, tree barks, wooden
fencing, perhaps carved inscriptions
and embellishments on buildings and,
if you are lucky, one of the old
fashioned cast-iron cellar covers
which are already collectors' pieces.
All these items will give satisfactory
rubbings if you lay a piece of paper
on the surface, hold it in place with
one hand, and with the other hold a
crayon flat on its side and rub it
firmly over the paper, always
following the same direction. As you
become confident, you will be able
to perform this operation deftly to
make a clear replica of the surface
beneath the paper. You will not have
to walk far to make quite a collection
of rubbings which can be cut up and
arranged in many interesting ways.

Most textured surfaces are suitable
for this work. The cards here were all
made up from rubbings of embossed
wallpapers. The rubbings were cut up
into rectangles or shapes which
closely followed the form of the
pattern and the pieces were mounted
on card and decorated with strips of
gold paper, sequins and washers.

Using this technique, explore the
possibilities of building decorative
houses or animals from different
textures, shapes and colours.

77, 78

79

43

Metallic Paper Impressions

80, 81

Metal foil (kitchen type is fine)
Thick wad of blotting paper
Pencil
Pair of scissors
Adhesive
Mounting card

Most metals are malleable, that is they can be formed by hammering or other forms of pressure. Metal foil is aluminium which is so thin that it can be distorted by the pressure of a pencil. If a thick sheet of blotting paper or something similarly soft, is placed under the foil, a three-dimensional metal drawing can be made with a pencil point. Various thicknesses of line and texture can be achieved — experimentation is the rule. When the drawing is complete it can be cut out and mounted on stiff paper. Apply the adhesive thickly as it will help to stiffen the form and make the drawing more durable. Metal foil is very delicate and likely to become marked or crumpled unless great care is taken.

The two cards were designed and made by fourteen-year-old children in the College Industriel de Levallois.

Spray Silhouettes

82

Paint
Old toothbrush
Ruler or similar flat material
Paper
Scissors
Dressmaking pins
Adhesive
Mounting card

Splatter pictures can be made by applying colour to an old tooth-brush which is then held in front of a sheet of paper and the surface of the brush scraped with a ruler or other flat tool. If the colour is fairly thick and the scraping is done along the surface of the brush towards the operator (away from the picture), it is possible to obtain an even splatter surface on the picture. By cutting paper silhouettes and pinning them to the surface of the painting prior to the splattering, you will obtain clear, self-coloured shapes on your picture. This work should be performed when the picture is propped vertically and surrounding surfaces are protected to prevent accidental splashing.

Fig. 82 was built up by splattering round the same shape four times, pinned in four different positions, and the design completed by the addition of the silhouette itself.

Figs. 83 and 84 show a card along with all the different shapes which were used to build up the picture.

The cards were made by thirteen- and fourteen-year-old children at the Lycée de Courbevoie.

Designs can be built up by using cut-out paper shapes and ready-made shapes such as fancy keys and other hardware, paper doilies, open-weave fabrics and laces, and decorative threads. Make a collection of likely materials which could be useful in other fields, say, print-making.

45

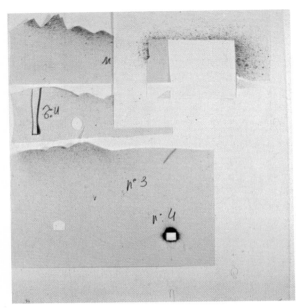

83

84

Ink Runs

85–7

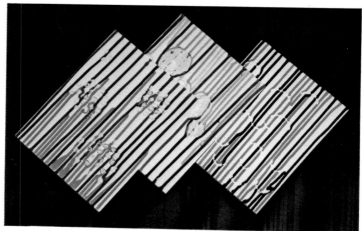

88–90

Coloured inks
Paint brush
Wax crayons
Stiff mounting card

To practise making ink runs, hold a piece of paper almost vertically and from a fully loaded paint brush, put a blob of ink near the top edge of the paper. The ink will run down the sheet and by tipping the paper to various angles, you will find that it is possible to control the direction of the runs.

Ink cannot take to paper which has been waxed, so that if you draw wax crayon lines and shapes before the ink is applied, you will obtain interestingly distorted runs. A few of the possibilities are shown here.

When making a card, work on a piece of paper slightly larger than your requirements for the finished card, so that the beginnings and the ends of the runs can be trimmed off to obtain a neat design.

47

91–6

Shaped Cards

Coloured paper/cardboard
Scissors

When cutting out freely shaped
cards, there are two things that must
be remembered. Assuming that you
start off with a folded rectangular
card, take care

1 to leave a large percentage of the
   folded edge intact, otherwise the
   card may not hold together

and

2 to leave a large percentage of the
   base intact, otherwise the card
   may topple over.

Test the card at regular intervals
during the cutting to make sure that
its stands correctly.

The cards opposite are suggestions
for a garden party, tea party, house-
warming party etc., but there are lots
more possibilities, for example, a
record party, fancy dress party or a
wine and cheese party.

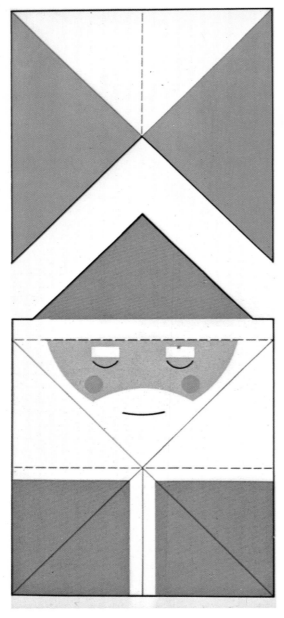

97

3D Cards

Thin card
Knife
Ruler
Any colouring materials you may
choose

The cards illustrated here are slightly
more difficult to construct than those
shown earlier. Although a plan (fig.
97) is given for the manufacture of
the Father Christmas (fig. 102) and
the butterfly (fig. 98), it is not
envisaged that the reader will mass
produce cards from these, but that he
will work them through as an exercise
and, when he is familiar with the
technique, will make his own designs.

All fold lines should be scored with a
sharp knife as described on p. 9.
Remember to score on the appropriate side of the paper, depending
which way you need to make the
fold.

A rewarding shape for experiment is a
square of thin cardboard folded first
in half, then into quarters, opened
out and re-folded along the diagonals
(fig. 99). The resultant form can be
developed into all kinds of struc-
tures. Play around with a number of
similar forms and see what you can
make.

Colouring can be added by painting,
crayoning or other methods you may
feel are suitable for your design.
Instant colour, black ink and
coloured papers were used on the
designs illustrated.

98

100, 101

102

103

104

Lettering

Greetings cards which contain no lettering, either inside or on the front, can be perfectly acceptable and complete in themselves. But once you become really involved in card-making, there will be times when you will wish to produce your own, formally designed message.

There are many ways of doing this, and we often fail to realize how appealing attractive handwriting can be if it is well presented and written in a strong black or coloured ink (figs. 113–16). It is advisable to write the inscription in rough at first, so that the border widths can be ascertained, to make a well-balanced page. Take time over the lay-out, for if it is not perfect, the simplest design can be ruined. Always write on some kind of guide line, usually a faint pencil line which can be cleaned off when the lettering is finished.

You could cut out a printed greeting from an old card and mount it on your design. However, it may be difficult to find just the right greeting, in the style and size of lettering you want. There is also the problem of matching the paper on which it is printed with the paper from which your card is made.

Another method is to cut out individual letters from a magazine and mount them in the order required. The snag with this is that you invariably run short of the odd letter and are unable to complete the message. Also, it is difficult to cut out letters really neatly. It is possible to overcome these difficulties and make an attractive display by assembling words from more than one style of letter.

It is useful to master an easy method of lettering with which you can design messages to suit your specific requirements. The chart drawn on squared graph paper shows some methods of drawing basic letter forms. A fibre tipped pen which draws a line width suitable for the size of letter, is all that is required for pages and pages of practising. When you are proficient, you will find thousands of uses for your skill.

It is unwise to practise lettering on a small scale. We recommend that you start off on graph paper with a minimum sized square of 5 mm [$\frac{1}{4}$ in].

1 These are lower case letters, most of which fill one square exactly. (Exceptions i, j, l and w.) If you lack sufficient confidence to begin with the whole alphabet, try to get the feel of making the shapes by drawing a whole row of o's, for o is the basis of most of these letter forms. First put a small dot to mark the centre of each side of one of the squares. This will give a guide when shaping the letter, which should touch the

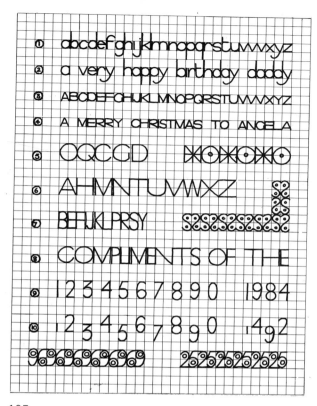

① abcdefghijklmnopqrstuvwxyz
② a very happy birthday daddy
③ ABCDEFGHIJKLMNOPQRSTUVWXYZ
④ A MERRY CHRISTMAS TO ANGELA
⑤ OQCGD KOKOKO
⑥ AHMNTUVWXZ
⑦ BEFIJKLPRSY
⑧ COMPLIMENTS OF THE
⑨ 1 2 3 4 5 6 7 8 9 0 1984
⑩ 1 2 3 4 5 6 7 8 9 0 1492

105

106
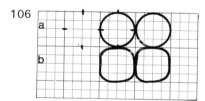

107 HERE'S WISHING YOU A
HARROWING HALLOWEEN

sides of the square only at the point of the dots and not as shown in fig. 106b.

Next, attempt to draw, freehand, the whole alphabet making the letters as round, full and simple in form as you can. Repeat the task until you are satisfied with the results, noting which of the letter tails extend a full square in length, and which do not.

2 Now try writing phrases, leaving one square vacant for the space between the words.

3 A row of upper case letters which are the same widths as the letters in 2. These should be easy to copy, but the result will not be as refined as it might be, as the most elegant upper case letters are not all the same widths.

5, 6, 7 An upper case alphabet which is roughly based on the classic Roman alphabet. This alphabet is divisible into three basic letter widths (exceptions I and J which are only the width of the pen line).

5 Letters based on a circle.

6 Letters based on a square.

7 Letters based on half the width of a square (except I and J).

8 Letters from the previous three rows used in a phrase.

9 The simplest proportions of numerals.

10 A more sophisticated positioning of 9 on the line.

108

The spaces on the chart are filled
with decorative borders derived from
letter and number forms.

As soon as you begin to feel confident at writing all these forms on
squared paper, try to execute the
same proportions of letters on
ordinary lined, writing paper. By
using the full space between the
lines, you will have a height guide for
the letters.

Now you will be able to use this skill
in designing your own cards. Plan
the design on rough paper first. Use
guide lines ruled on the card, making
sure that they are at right angles
with the edge of the card, and clean
them off when the lettering is
finished and the ink is dry.

109

Lettering

Figs. 108 and 109 show the use of the lettering described on the previous two pages. The lettering and border should be planned on squared paper first and if it is drawn with strong black ink, it should be possible to see the design on the reverse side of the paper. In order to transfer the design to the foil, you must work on top of a soft wad of newspaper or blotting paper. Put the foil on this and then the squared paper with the lettering face downwards. Hold the papers in place with a little masking tape and then trace the lettering very heavily with the pointed, wooden end of a paint brush. The pressure will give you raised letters and patterns on the foil. Remove the tape, cut the foil design neatly to shape and mount with plenty of adhesive on whatever background you find suitable. The adhesive will give support to the rather fragile letters.

This method gives a very exotic looking card for special occasions.

PLEASE COME TO

OUR PARTY

ON JUNE 6TH AT 7PM

RSVP

110

111

CONGRATULATIONS

ON YOUR

SILVER WEDDING ANNIVERSARY

ANNIE & TREVOR

Interiers

Interiors

112

Paper/cardboard
Ruler
Pencil
Writing pen and ink (or ball point
pen)

A well-considered lay-out of
ordinary handwriting which is neatly
executed, can look attractive on a
greetings card, as figs. 113–16 show.
Variety can be obtained with
different thicknesses of pen and with
more than one size of writing on one
design. Later on, when you have
gained confidence and experience,
it would be worth while investing in
a special italic lettering pen. The
lettering in fig. 112 is an example of
what can be achieved with practice.
Always rule lines before commencing
work and plan the lettering as
described on p. 54.

With a little care, most beautiful
cards can be produced.

All the card designs on this page are
by Ron Welsh.

113

R.S.V.P. – 2 Smith Rd., East Cheam.

Mr. & Mrs. Davington-Smyth
request the pleasure of the company of
MR. & MRS. JOHN BROWN
at the wedding of their daughter Cynthia
to Mr. Eric Little, on Saturday,
15th August, at S. Swithin's Church,
East Cheam, at 2.00 p.m.

114

Heartiest congratulations
and best wishes
for your Silver Wedding
Pam & John.

115

Get well soon
All of us are looking
forward to having you
back with us again.
Joseph

116

Janet and John proudly announce
the arrival of SIMON NICHOLAS
born on Wednesday (14th July) —
all 7 lbs. 5 ozs. of him!

Instant Dry Lettering

117, 118

Coloured papers
Instant dry lettering

Professional lettering can be obtained by using transfer instant letters which are now manufactured by several firms.

The letters are on waxy sheets which, when rubbed with a blunt point, release the letters onto the card.

When not in use, the backing sheet which is supplied with the letters must be kept in place. This ensures that the letters do not pick up dust which would prevent them sticking when applied to the card or paper.

The two cards illustrated were designed using Blick 'Dry Print'. Other makes obtainable are Letraset, Letter-Press and Alfac.

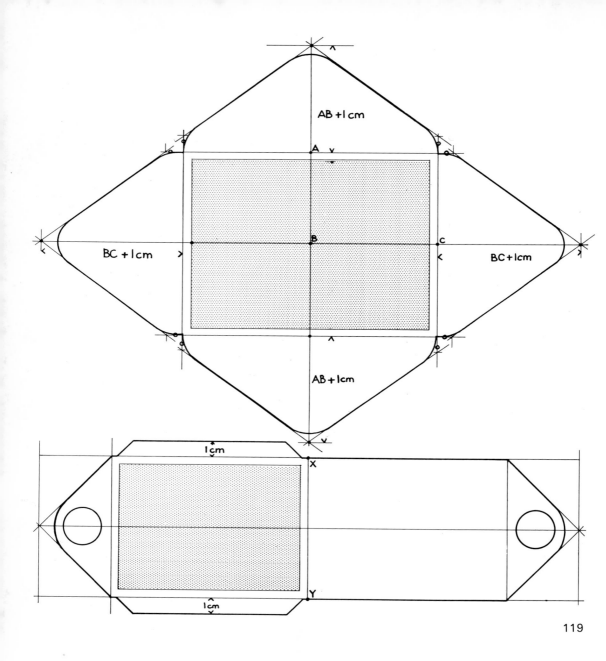

AB +1cm

A

BC + 1cm

B

c

BC +1cm

AB +1cm

1cm

X

1cm

Y

119

60

Envelopes

Paper
Scissors
Ruler
Pencil

Before designing cards, it is advisable to go to a good stationery shop to find out what sizes of envelopes are available, then design your cards to fit them. Sometimes you may wish to make a card of unconventional proportions for which a special envelope must be made, or you would like an envelope to be made of paper to match a card, or you may wish to make a highly decorative envelope — Victorian style.

The two diagrams will give you a guide to envelope making. The shaded part of the diagram indicates the size of the card to be covered and the heavy lines are the ones along which to cut out your envelope.

NB Because of the introduction of automatic stamping machines, postal authorities are becoming particular about the sizes and proportions of envelopes. Any which do not conform may be subject to extra charge.

Some Occasions for Sending Cards

Birthdays
  including
  Fathers
  Mothers
  Sisters etc.
  Individual names
  and Special Birthdays —
  1, 2, 3, 4 etc., and 18 and 21

Bon Voyage

Congratulations on
  Coming of Age
  Engagement
  Passing Exams
  Winning the Competition

Get Well

Good luck
  Exams
  Trips

Happy Anniversary
  Christmas
  Easter
  Father's Day
  Hallowe'en
  Mother's Day
  New Year
  Valentine's Day

I'm Sorry I Forgot
  Anniversary
  Birthday

Information Cards
  Change of Address
  Closing down
  Going away
  Moving House

Invitations to
  Dinner
  Outing
  Parties
  Picnics
  Tea
  Theatre

Thank you for
  Looking after the Children/House/
  Pets
  The Dinner
  The Party
  The Present
  Your Help

Welcome Back

Well Done

Wishing You Well
  In the New House
  In the New Job
  On the Voyage

Suppliers

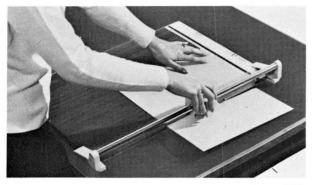

120

Good shops selling art and craft materials should stock all the papers, paints, adhesives and tools mentioned in the text.

Britain
There is one particularly good shop stocking a wide range of plain and fancy papers, by the sheet:
Paper Chase, Tottenham Court Road, London.

Educational Departments requiring quantities of tools and materials should contact one of the Educational Suppliers such as

Dryad, Northgates, Leicester.

Margros, Monument Way West, Woking, Surrey.

Winsor and Newton Ltd., Weald-stone, Harrow, Middlesex.

Reeves, Lincoln Road, Enfield, Middlesex.

All these firms stock full ranges of materials and equipment.

Sequins, ribbons and buttons can be purchased from needlework shops such as

John Lewis Ltd., Oxford Street, London.

The Needlewoman, Regent Street, London.

Tiny washers and other ironmongery will be found in hardware shops.

The Platignum Spot Stick is an asset in fine work. Most stationery shops stock this item but if you have difficulty in obtaining one, write to Platignum Ltd., Schools Division, Six Hills Way, Stevenage, Hertfordshire.

The Myers Trimmer illustrated is an excellent machine for anyone who wishes to do a great deal of paper cutting. It saves hours of work which would otherwise have to be carried out laboriously with a square and knife. The results obtained with it are most professional. It is safe for use by children. Supplied by M. Myers and Son Ltd., Oldbury, Warley, Worcs.

USA
A wide range of plain and fancy papers will be found at
Andrews, Nelson, Whitehead, Boise, 7 Laight St., New York, NY 10013.

Educational departments requiring quantities of tools and materials should contact:
The Craftool Company, Wood-Ridge, New Jersey 07075.

Sequins, ribbons, and buttons can be purchased from:
Sol Kahaner and Bro., 55 West 38th St., New York, NY 10018.

Dennison Manufacturing Co., 370 Lexinton Ave., New York, NY 10017.

You can get the Pastemaker glue pen at any art-supply store such as: Joseph Mayer Co., Inc., 845 Broadway, New York, NY 10003.

A paper cutting machine is also available from:
Joseph Mayer Co., Inc., 845 Broadway, New York, NY 10003.

Arthur Brown & Bro., Inc., 2 West 46th St., New York, NY 10036.

Where examples of greetings cards can be seen
Greetings cards are becoming collectors' pieces and many museums have small but rapidly growing collections of early examples — in particular the Castle Museum, York, and the Victoria and Albert Museum, South Kensington, London. The latter has a large collection which can be viewed on request.

In the USA: Metropolitan Museum, 5th Ave., and 82nd St., New York City; and New York Public Library, 5th Ave. and 42nd St., New York City.

Bibliography

Batsford Books (Creative Play Series)

Röttger, Ernst. *Creative Paper Craft* (1961).

Röttger, Ernst and Klante, Dieter. *Creative Drawing* (1964).

Kampmann, Lothar. *Pictures with Coloured Paper* (1968).
  Pictures with Paints (1968).
  Pictures with Crayons (1968).
  Pictures with Inks (1969).
  Picture Printing (1969).

Arundell, Jan and Southwell, Ray. *Design and Make Prints* (Dent, 1975).

Carlis, John. *How to Make Your Own Greeting Cards* (Watson-Guptill, 1968).